FOR MY SHIMMY MOTHER & SHIMMY FATHER AND PATRICK THE SHIMMY-SHAKE-IT KING!

Compilation copyright © 1992 by Cynthia Jabar
Illustrations copyright © 1992 by Cynthia Jabar

First Edition

Acknowledgments
Thanks are given to the following for permission to reprint copyrighted material: **Theodore Clymer**: "The little blackbirds are singing . . ." from *Four Corners of the Sky* (1975). Reprinted by permission of Little, Brown and Company. **Nikki Giovanni**: "Dance Poem" from *Spin a Soft Black Song* by Nikki Giovanni. Copyright © 1971, 1985 by Nikki Giovanni. Reprinted by permission of Farrar, Straus and Giroux, Inc. **Langston Hughes**: "Dream Boogie" copyright 1951 by Langston Hughes. Copyright renewed 1979 by George Houston Bass. Reprinted by permission of Harold Ober Associates, Inc. **Margaret Mahy**: "The Man from the Land of Fandango" from *Nonstop Nonsense* by Margaret Mahy. Copyright © 1977 by Margaret Mahy. Reprinted with permission of J. M. Dent & Sons Ltd. and Margaret K. McElderry Books, an imprint of Macmillan Publishing Company. **Lillian Morrison**: "B Boy" from *The Break Dance Kids* by Lillian Morrison. Copyright © 1985 by Lillian Morrison. Reprinted by permission of William Morrow and Company. **Ogden Nash**: "Russian Dance" from *Custard and Company* by Ogden Nash. Copyright © 1961, 1962 by Ogden Nash. Reprinted with permission of Little, Brown and Company and Curtis Brown Ltd. **Nina Payne:** "Fancy Dancer" from *All the Day Long* by Nina Payne. Copyright © 1973 by Nina Payne. Reprinted by permission of Atheneum, an imprint of Macmillan Publishing Company. **Jack Prelutsky**: "Forty Performing Bananas" from *New Kid on the Block* by Jack Prelutsky. Copyright © 1984 by Jack Prelutsky. Reprinted by permission of Greenwillow Books, William Morrow and Company, and William Heinemann Ltd. "Parrot with a pomegranate . . ." from *Ride a Purple Pelican* by Jack Prelutsky. Copyright © 1986 by Jack Prelutsky. Reprinted by permission of William Morrow and Company. **Thomas Rockwell**: "Rackety-Bang" copyright © 1969 by Thomas Rockwell. Reprinted by permission of Thomas Rockwell and Raines & Raines. **Geoffrey Summerfield:** "Tap-Dancing" from *Welcome and Other Poems* by Geoffrey Summerfield. Copyright © 1983 by Geoffrey Summerfield. Reprinted by permission of Andre Deutsch Ltd.

Library of Congress Cataloging-in-Publication Data

Shimmy shake earthquake : don't forget to dance poems / collected and
   illustrated by Cynthia Jabar. — 1st ed.
      p.   cm.
      Summary: Poems of Jack Prelutsky, Margaret Mahy, Ogden Nash,
and others reflect a broad ethnic background and the rhythms and
sounds of dance.
      ISBN 0-316-43459-0
      1. Children's poetry, American. 2. Dancing — Juvenile literature.
[1. Poetry — Collections.   2. Dancing.]   I. Jabar, Cynthia.
PS586.3.S5   1992
811' .5080355—dc20   91-18305

Joy Street Books are published by Little, Brown and Company (Inc.)

10 9 8 7 6 5 4 3 2 1

NIL

Published simultaneously in Canada by Little, Brown & Company (Canada) Limited

Printed in Italy

SHIMMY SHAKE EARTHQUAKE

Don't Forget to Dance Poems

Collected and Illustrated by Cynthia Jabar

JOY STREET BOOKS

LITTLE, BROWN AND COMPANY
BOSTON   TORONTO   LONDON

THE MAN FROM THE LAND OF FANDANGO

The man from the land of Fandango
Is coming to pay you a call,
With his tricolor jacket and polka-dot tie
And his calico trousers as blue as the sky
And a hat with a tassel and all.
And he bingles and bangles and bounces,
He's a bird! He's a bell! He's a ball!
The man from the land of Fandango
Is coming to pay you a call.
Oh, whenever they dance in Fandango
The bears and the bison join in,
And the baboons with bassoons make a musical sound,
And the kangaroos come with a hop and a bound,
And the dinosaurs join in the din,
And they tingle and tongle and tangle
Till tomorrow turns into today.
Then they stop for a break and a drink and a cake
In their friendly fandandical way.

The man from the land of Fandango
Is given to dancing and dreams.
He comes in at the door like a somersault star
And he juggles with junkets and jam in a jar
And custards and caramel creams.
And he jingles and jongles and jangles
As he dances on ceilings and walls,
And he appears every five hundred years
So you'd better be home when he calls.

Margaret Mahy

BOOGIE CHANT AND DANCE

Ladies and gentlemen and children, too,
Here are four nice girls gonna boogie for you.
They're gonna turn around,
They're gonna touch the ground,
They're gonna shake their shoulders
Till the sun goes down.
Hands up! Ha-ha. Ha-ha-ha!
Hands down! Ha-ha. Ha-ha-ha!
Got a penny, call Jack Benny. Ha-ha. Ha-ha-ha!
Got a nickle, buy a pickle. Ha-ha. Ha-ha-ha!
Got a dime, ain't it fine. Ha-ha. Ha-ha-ha!

Traditional

DREAM BOOGIE

Good-morning, daddy!
Ain't you heard
The boogie-woogie rumble
Of a dream deferred?

Listen closely:
You'll hear their feet
Beating out and beating out a —
You think
It's a happy beat?

Listen to it closely:
Ain't you heard
something underneath
like a —
What did I say?

Sure,
I'm happy!
Take it away!

Hey, pop!
Re-bop!
Mop!

Y-e-a-h!

Langston Hughes

B BOY

As onlookers clap
and rap and shout
I curl up and turn myself
inside out.

I can jig horizontal
as I lean on one hand;
I'm a spin-top, a pinwheel,
a one-man dance band,

inventing new moves
When I get a notion,
I can take out the best.
I'm graffiti in motion,

a sidewalk tornado
to the rhythm of rock
Meet the baddest break dancer
(that's me) on the block.

Lillian Morrison

SHIMMY SHAKE IT!

Shimmy shake it,
Do everything but break it!

Flip it, flop it,
She hip-hop it.

So much fun,
We can't stop it!

Jump it, twirl it,
Dip'n curl it,
Twist'n shout it —
YELL about it!

Cynthia Jabar

The High Skip,
The Sly Skip,
The Skip like a Feather,
The Long Skip,
The Strong Skip,
The Skip All Together!

The Slow Skip,
The Toe Skip,
The Skip Double-Double,
The Fast Skip,
The Last Skip,
And the Skip Against Trouble!

Mother Goose

To market, to market, to buy a fat pig,
Home again, home again, dancing a jig.
To market, to market, to buy a fat hog,
Home again, home again, jiggety-jog.

Mother Goose

FORTY PERFORMING BANANAS

We're forty performing bananas,
in bright yellow slippery skins,
our features are rather appealing,
though we've neither shoulders nor chins,
we cha-cha, fandango, and tango,
we kick and we skip and we hop,
while half of us belt out a ballad,
the rest of us spin like a top.

We're forty performing bananas,
we mambo, we samba, we waltz,
we dangle and swing from the ceiling,
then turn very slick somersaults,
people drive here in bunches to see us,
our splits earn us worldly renown,
we're forty performing bananas,
come see us when you are in town.

Jack Prelutsky

RUSSIAN DANCE

The Russian moujik is made for music,
For music the moujik is most enthusic,
Whenever an instrument twangs or toots
He tucks his trousers into his boots,
He squats on his heels, but his knees don't crack,
And he kicks like a frenzied jumping jack.
My knees would make this performance tragic,
But his have special moujik magic.

Ogden Nash

RACKETY-BANG

Loose-limbed Cindy
danced the lindy
upstairs, downstairs,
in her brother's highchair,
along the top of the garden bench,
back and forth across the trench,
in and out of the county jail,
rackety-bang on a garbage pail,
    to school —
  where she sat
  quiet as a cat
    and learned
    and learned
    and learned
    and learned
    and learned
    and learned
    and learned
    and learned —
till three o'clock,
when at the shock
  of the bell,

she danced around, around the janitor's pail,
in and out of a rummage sale,
back and forth across the trench,
along the top of a picket fence,
in all the chairs,
upstairs, downstairs,
then into the shed
to eat her gingerbread.

Thomas Rockwell

TAP-DANCING
for Liberty Blake

Antics in the attics,
Antics in the cellars,
Upstairs and downstairs,
Tap-dancing fellahs!

Bill Bojangles, Buck and Bubbles,
Tap your way through all your troubles!
Bunny and Sandman, Chuckles and Chuck,
Dance your way through all kinds of luck!

Tap your toes and tap your heels,
Let us know how the tapdancer feels!
Tiptop in the morning, toptoe at night,
Tap toes and heels till we all come out right!

I can do the cancan
    just like this.
I can do the Hula-Hoop,
I can do the twist.
Queens go curtsy,
Kings go bow,
Boys go, "Hi there!"
Girls go, "Wow!"

Traditional

FANCY DANCE

Teach myself so[m]
fancy dances,

flash my feet and
take my chances.

Soon as I giggle
my belly will jigg[le]

Soon as I leap
I'll fall in a heap.

Soon as I rise
I'll cross my eyes

Soon as I'm thro[ugh]
I'll dance with yo[u]

Nina Payne

Tap to your funeral, tap into the ground,
Tap up to heaven and look around!
Tap Saint Peter and his bunch of keys,
Tap Old Gabriel if you please!
Tap toe and heel every cloud-capped tower
Tap every cloud till it runs a shower!
Tap the old sun for solar power
Tap it to the earth, open every flower!
Tap in the thunder and tap in the rain
Tap till the whole world rings again!

One two, three four five,
Tap again till you feel alive!
Six, seven, eight nine ten,
Tap for all you're worth, then tap again!
Seven, eight, nine ten eleven,
Tap for the earth and tap for heaven!

Geoffrey Summerfield

Parrot with a pomegranate,
pigeon with a peach,
flew to Honolulu
to dance upon the beach,
they danced a pair of polkas,
they danced a polonaise,
then ended with a hula,
and slept for seven days.

Jack Prelutsky

LEAP AND DANCE

The lion walks on padded paws,
The squirrel leaps from limb to limb,
While flies can crawl straight up a wall,
And seals can dive and swim.
The worm, it wiggles all around,
The monkey swings by its tail,
And birds may hop upon the ground,
Or spread their wings and sail.
But boys and girls have much more fun;
They leap and dance
And walk
And run.

Anonymous

DANCE POEM

come nataki dance with me
bring your pablum dance with me
pull your plait and whorl around
come nataki dance with me

won't you tony dance with me
stop your crying dance with me
feel the rhythm of my arms
don't let's cry now dance with me

tommy stop your tearing up
don't you hear the music
don't you feel the happy beat
don't bite tony dance with me
mommy needs a partner

here comes karma she will dance
pirouette and bugaloo
short pink dress and dancing shoes
karma wants to dance with me
don't you karma don't you

all you children gather round
we will dance and we will whorl
we will dance to our own song
we must spin to our own world
we must spin a soft Black song
all you children gather round
we will dance together

Nikki Giovanni

THE BLACK TURKEY-GOBBLER

The black turkey-gobbler, under the East, the middle of his
    tail toward us; it is about to dawn.
The black turkey-gobbler, the tips of his beautiful tail;
    above us the dawn whitens.
The black turkey-gobbler, the tips of his beautiful tail;
    above us the dawn becomes yellow.
The sunbeams stream forward, dawn boys, with shimmering shoes
    of yellow;
On top of the sunbeams that stream toward us they are
    dancing.
At the East the rainbow moves forward, dawn maidens, with
    shimmering shoes and shirts of yellow dance over us.
Beautifully over us it is dawning.

Traditional, Mescalero Apache

The little blackbirds are singing this song as they dance
around the four corners of the sky.

Traditional, Yuma